# The Dental Success Secret

## To Having a Vibrant Practice
## That Thrives and Grows
### Year After Year After Year

# THE DENTAL SUCCESS SECRET

### To Having a Vibrant Practice
### That Thrives and Grows
### Year after Year after Year

## Scott J. Manning, MBA

# COPYRIGHT

# OUR MISSION

## Scott J. Manning, MBA, and Dental Success Today

We are committed to serve, save, and embolden the Independent Dentist. Our goal is to empower dentists to reclaim their right to practice as they wish, to earn what they deserve, and to create a lifestyle and dental business of their own design. We do this by providing the tools they need to proliferate their philosophy toward the health and care of patients who are committed to investing to achieve optimal health, and who value the dentist's talent, skills, integrity, and quality of care. We believe that meeting these goals will allow the dentist to continue learning, growing and solving new clinical challenges that will provide patients with the ultimate in dental health care, while ultimately allowing the dentist to build wealth and enjoy a fuller life.

"You cannot expect to achieve new goals
or move beyond your present circumstances
unless you change."
– *Les Brown*

# SOMEDAY

The fact you are reading this book proves you are one of a very select group. How do I know? Because most dentists wait until it's too late to figure out what they want out of their practice. It's never NOW, it's always SOMEDAY off in the future.

- Someday they'll decide when they want to retire.
- Someday they'll figure out how much money they want to put away.
- Someday they'll determine the way in which they'd prefer to work, practice, and do dentistry.

Most don't have a plan for their practice. They simply show up every day and deal with whomever happens to be in the schedule. And because they have no plan they accept whatever revenue the schedule provides at the end of the day.

Now, I don't think you're like this. After all, you're smart, forward thinking, future–focused, and have standards. You took the time and initiative to request this book and you're taking the time right now to review and carefully consider its contents. You aren't willing to simply settle for the status quo.

But, being aware doesn't mean that time won't catch up with you. You can still be accepting less than you deserve. You may not be living every day in your practice totally fulfilled, passionate, and focused, with every skill and talent fully utilized.

Make today the day you take action! Turn "someday" into "today."

# Table of Contents

# Table of Contents
## — Continued —

# INTRODUCTION

The point of being in business for yourself is to have a practice that you control so you can fulfill your dreams. But, there is a secret to having a vibrant practice that thrives and continues to grow year after year. In this book I will share information that you can use to experience a dramatic increase in profits by leveraging assets you already have in place. I'm going to dive deep and actually work with you to make this secret come to life in your practice.

If you're looking for an easy button, it's not here. But, if you're looking for the "money button," the ATM machine to your practice that keeps on giving again, and again, and again, then you're in the right place. And if you want to make it so that it feels effortless and you can enjoy and be invigorated by the process of being in professional practice for yourself, you'll find the key in this book.

What does that mean to you? It means you can experience the fulfillment of having a practice that operates on your terms. A practice that provides not only the high level of professional quality service your patients desire, but a practice that delivers the kind of lifestyle you and those whom you love deserve. We can work together to create the practice of your dreams, not mine. I don't want to force something down your throat. I don't want to sell you the next "bag of goods." I will not tell you to do anything that interferes with what you believe and want your practice to be about.

Others who have come before me have no doubt tried to make you "them," so that they can convince you to buy whatever they're selling and lead you down a path that you probably don't want to go down. The practice that will work for you is the practice that you want to have.

I'm here as your coach, your partner, and your friend to advise, encourage, and yes, my favorite part, kick you in the ass as needed in order to get the kind of results from your business that you want. I'm not going to hold you to any standard that I wouldn't hold myself to. We're in this together from start to finish.

# ABOUT SCOTT J. MANNING, MBA

My experience has been across North America, with all varieties of practices, including specialty practices; general practices, solo; boutique-style concierge practices; mega-multi doctor, but single owner practices; and general practices.

I see more patients and more practices in a week than you could in a lifetime, and that allows me to have great insight and understanding. I don't have a narrow view and I am not judgmental. I see the many facets of this great industry and that's what gives me the ability, the experience, and the credibility to serve.

I believe that at the end of the day there is only one person that matters, and that's you. You get to choose the vision for your practice that is right for you.

I'm very passionate about this. I am dedicated to bringing your dreams to life.

My other books contain more complete background information so I won't go into a lot of detail about myself here. But there are a couple of things you should know.

First of all, I'm not a dentist—I am an expert in dream fulfillment.

I won't try to change you—the last thing on earth you need is someone else trying to convince you that you need to change who you are. Instead, I will give you the tools and knowledge to create the practice of your dreams. Because, in the real world your business (and your practice IS a business) will only be as great as your understanding of the business skills you need in order to develop the practice that you deserve to have.

You need someone in your corner who has mastered the business side of dentistry like no one else, someone who does not resort to a cookie-cutter system or a one-size-fits-all plan. My vast business experience in the dental industry gives you peace of mind because you know that I can serve you.

I tease my doctors that I like dentistry more than they do, but perhaps that's part of their problem. So many doctors come to the point you have now because they're searching. They are hungry to be reinvigorated about their practice.

This often happens after they wander off the range, out into the wilderness of commoditized, discount, insurance-driven dentistry. They're fighting a battle they do not want to fight and probably can't win, and they want to find a way to restore their passion.

Other doctors appreciate my passion because they are also passionate about what they do. The have an amazing practice doing exactly the kind of things they choose to help change the lives of the patients that they see and they want to take it to the next level.

**What People Say — Kind Comments About Scott**

These are a few of the kind comments we've received from other doctors who have been through the planning process with me. Dr. William Swan says, "*This guy is wonderful. Probably one of the most brilliant people I've met thus far.*" Of course I would like to remove "probably", because certainly my expectation is to be *the* most.

Dr. Browning is from Texas. He said, "*He knows his stuff. Very knowledgeable. He's got the experience. A brilliant guy and a great teacher.*" Well, isn't that who you would want in your corner?

Now, I would also like to mention this very nice person, Dr. Bannan from North Carolina. He said, "*I think Scott is an excellent coach to help you get where you want to go as you figure out where that is.*" That's what we're going to work on in this book.

So let's get started!

# CHAPTER 1
## Rate Your Reality

**8**    Chapter 1

# Chapter 1
## Rate Your Reality

Before we get started with the material, I want you to think honestly about what your vision is for your life and your practice and how close your current reality matches that vision. Then I want you to rate them together on a scale from 1 to 10. You are the only one seeing this, so be totally honest.

In this rating, give yourself a "1" if you feel completely incompetent, negligent, or nonexistent and you wake up every day disgusted with the practice that you have to walk into. You may feel this way about your financial results right now, or your team, or your patients, or your dentistry, or just your life outside your practice.

Give yourself a "10" if you think you are a "Rock Star." Of course, Rock Star is perfection, the perfect state of ideal. You think, "I cannot possibly consider changing anything there is." This means your life and practice is at a point where every day is exactly the way you want it. You're earning what you expect, not working a minute more than you wish, and you have all the peace you can cram into your mind.

So, we go from a state of ideal perfection down to absolutely nothing that you want to keep at all, you want to blow it up and start over. So, gauge where you're at on that scale. Don't think of anyone else right now, just your own viewpoint.

By the way, if you give yourself a 10, you shouldn't continue with this process. Go do something else. Not because you're already perfect, we both know that's not possible. Stop, because it's clear you aren't critical enough and you are most certainly settling for far less than is possible in your practice. It's one thing to be a happy person, but another to be so content you lack ambition and, therefore, purpose.

I want you to circle your rating now. Remember, life is never about what you've achieved. It's about the potential of what could be. That's how people think who sacrifice and invest in themselves and their future.

### Where Am I Now?

1   2   3   4   5   6   7   8   9   10

So, how did you do? Very few dentists say they have total control over their outcomes. Very few are creating deliberate growth and have a plan they use to guide their practice forward. I'm talking about a career plan that begins with the lifestyle they want to have and uses other elements to create that lifestyle. A few of these include:

- Wealth building
- Practice growth
- Team building
- Dentistry
- Budget
- Profit
- Expenses
- Schedule

These are all pillars that your practice, as a business, is built upon and …

- if they aren't planned out and orchestrated,
- if they aren't deliberately designed,
- if there is no reason why things happen,
- if there is no cause and effect to get the results you desire,
- if your goals are not met and your time is devalued,

...then, at some point you are going to end up frustrated as you find yourself behind in time or money (or both) and blocked by your team, or worse yet, your patients.

I don't say this to scare you. I say it because this is reality. In the Multi-Millionaire Club, we call this realization "healthy paranoia." Recognizing and embracing your own inner sense of "healthy paranoia" is the first step to making the changes you know deep down need to be made.

To help you make those changes happen as quickly as possible, I'm going to share a three-phase, proactive strategy that enables you to take full responsibility for getting exactly what you want in life, out of your practice and in dentistry, with your team and from your patients. It will involve some effort on your part. I make no apologies in that regard. Anything worth doing is worth doing right, right?

But have no fear. The "secret" to all of this is far easier than muddling along like you may well be doing right now—and I guarantee, the rewards both financially and emotionally are far greater.

You can choose to be just like some of your patients and live in a state of denial, waiting until the problem is so bad it has to be addressed. Or you can be a smart, responsible businessperson and get ahead of problems, prevent failures, and as a result achieve the optimal state of ideal—on purpose. That sounds magical.

- Business on purpose
- Dentistry on purpose
- Practicing on purpose
- Having fun on purpose
- Scheduling on purpose
- Diagnosing on purpose
- Leading your team on purpose

And all of this leads to my favorite part…

Getting RICH—On Purpose

Ultimately that's the point. You can pick the amount, you can write your own definition, because, ultimately you define what success means to you. Still, most will short-change themselves, not because they want to, but because they lack confidence, belief, and a structured process that leads to the results they deserve.

How much of this are you doing on purpose now? How much are you guided by your goals, mission, passion, profits—your purpose?

It is always surprising to me that so many doctors "take what they get" instead of designing an experience, practice and message to cultivate what they want. Many believe that the population in their location determines the kind of dentistry they are able to provide. I have to tell you, whether you're talking implants or dentures, scaling or surgery, you can find whatever dentistry you want to do in every city in America.

The question is, are you doing anything about it or just taking what falls in your lap? Why not create the kind of practice that invigorates you to wake up and get out of bed to run (not walk) into the office? A practice that makes you proud so you stand with your head up and voice strong? A practice that allows you to look into the eyes of your patients—and your team—to declare your conviction and belief in what you are doing to help other people?

Next, I will reveal the secret to creating the changes you need to make your vision a reality.

# DR. GERALD CIOFFI
## A Great Practice Becomes Awesome

"As a dental student at the University of Pennsylvania my focus became total care and consideration of oral manifestations of systemic disease.

"I completed a general practice residency in the Navy Dental Corp and a residency in general medicine at Bethesda Naval Hospital. I left the Navy in 1989 and set up a private practice in oral medicine in Orange Park, a suburb of Jacksonville, Florida, and I have been there ever since.

"My practice has served a definite need in the community and I have done very well. I built my practice more by doing continuing education for study groups, morning hospital groups, physician and dental groups, and specialty groups like the American Dental Association.

"I've done a lot of continuing education and lecturing. I also taught in the hygiene program at Florida State College in Jacksonville for about 27 years. Virtually every hygienist in Northeast Florida took my course, and they have been a reliable referral source over the years."

## But Something Was Missing

"My practice grew annually at an acceptable level until the economic crash in 2007 when a lot of practices that depended largely on discretionary money began to struggle.

"I got frustrated when some of my patients, particularly cancer patients, did not follow through with treatment. I decided that I must have failed to communicate with them enough. That realization inspired me to look for help.

"I had gone to numerous dental meetings and conferences, but I could never get comfortable with any of their programs, partly because they didn't fit with my own philosophy. I realized there could be better ways to operate my business that were still well within my personal beliefs and philosophy about my practice. I found what I was looking for in Dental Success Today."

### Making a Great Practice Awesome

"One of the things that attracted me to Dental Success Today was that instead of telling me to practice medicine differently, they simply asked me to pay more attention to how I was running my business. That was perfectly acceptable.

"I was very comfortable knowing that I would not have to change my approach to treating patients, diagnosis and treatment. Instead they would help me to do things better. I was attracted to the emphasis on communication and education, and systems and team building, because that was what I was missing."

## Change Can Be a Good Thing

"The whole staff participated in the first training session with Scott. To build a team, you've got to learn as a team. Training was very stimulating and invigorating for all of my team.

"Scott suggested we create the position of Treatment Coordinator. I needed someone who had both a business and medical background in this position. It turned out that person was my son. He had worked in home healthcare for five or six years, and he knew probably every physician in Northeast Florida as a result.

"Adding a Treatment Coordinator has been one of the most positive experiences of this whole program. It was a big change in my thinking and the practice and something we should have done 20 years ago."

## New Routines (Morning Huddles/Lunch & Learn)

"We now have 'morning huddles' and 'lunch and learn,' and other training. I always felt like what we did all day long was training, but it's not the same as planned training.

"The blueprint is big—there is a lot in it—and you have to keep implementing step by step and work things in. You allow time for the team to get used to new routines. We are less than a year yet into working the blueprint, but I've increased my practice 50 percent."

## New Freedom and Reduced Stress

"Last month we had one of the best months I've ever had and there were times when I felt like I really wasn't working. Everything was scheduled and executed so much better than we had done in the past. We are doing things better, smarter, more efficiently.

"2017 was the first year in my 30-year career that I have taken a week's vacation every quarter. My wife and I went to Venice, Italy, on our 47th anniversary, and we got on a ship and did the Greek Isles.

"Tomorrow I'm going to the Florida Keys for lobster season. The system gave me the confidence to create the schedule and know that I'm going to have the time off because it makes it achievable and doable."

### A Plan for the Future

"These positive changes have allowed me to finally think about the future. I enjoy what I'm doing, so I want to work my way out. I want to make—and take—more time, but I'm not going to walk away cold, and I need a plan for all that. Scott has given me a blueprint and we're starting to work on that now.

"I recently purchased the complex where my 5-chair practice is located and took a vacant suite next door to the practice. The new space will allow us to expand the office and make room for an associate. July 2021 is my target date for retirement. Following the blueprint, I can make the transition and not be stressed by it."

### Scott and Dental Success Came at the Right Time

"This program has provided me with the business tools and systems I needed to create positive growth. I'm not getting 6,000 new patients—we're doing much better with what we have.

"I'm moving forward and good things are happening professionally and personally. Moving forward is a victory and means more than anything else to me.

"When I found Scott and Dental Success Today, I was stuck. When I first saw the objectives and all the things that were going to happen, I thought, 'I sure hope it works, but I've got to see this to believe it.' Well, I believe it now because it's all happened."

**A Word to Those Who Need Help to Move Forward**

"You have to have a positive attitude about change. Everything I've done came right out of Scott's blueprint. That was key for me, because it was custom-designed for my practice and my philosophy.

"Scott's philosophy has been something I've been very comfortable with because we worked out my plan together. I told him what I needed and where I wanted to go and he told me how to do it. It has been a very, very positive change.

"It really can happen for you, too. You have to take one step at a time, keep the focus, and follow Scott's guidance. It will work. It works better and faster than I thought it would. If anyone has doubts and wants to talk to me, give me a call. I'm in the phone book."

# CHAPTER 2
## The Secret

# Chapter 2
## The Secret

There are many "secrets" in life, health, business, and leadership. Anyone who tells you there is only one thing you have to do, think, or believe is crazy. If achieving success is that easy everyone would do it.

But most people are complacent and satisfied with the status quo. They prefer boring and predictable to change, growth, and ambition. Predictable may be great when we are talking about wealth and retirement income but not when we are talking about business, leading people, getting rich and doing dentistry on your own terms. What is the greatest secret to having a vibrant practice that thrives and grows year after year?

Well, there's good news and bad news.

The secret I'm going to give you in this book is the foundation for everything else you will ever do or achieve.

Just this one secret alone has empowered the most successful, most sustainable, most profitable general practices in the world. This is the secret to your success, and to truly having the practice of your dreams. It is the secret to achieving more wealth in a shorter period of time. With this secret you can transition or exit at the top of your game for maximum value.

The secret to building an amazing team to achieve the dentistry you're passionate about, the schedule you want, and the income you deserve all comes down to these two words: Reverse Engineering.

This is far more important than you will realize until you actually embrace and own this concept, this technique, this way of doing business, leading, growing, making money, and practicing dentistry.

Now, I'm here to tell you—and I would know—no one does this. At least most dentists never think about taking their practice vision and working backwards down to the tiniest detail. Most dentists:

- live in the practice they have always known.

- just go through the motions year after year.

- want things but don't know how to actually make them happen.

Don't get me wrong, many dentists—you, I hope—have goals, and a vision. They have frustrations they would like to change and money they would like to make. But, it stops there. They get stuck in their daily routine. They make no progress, no proactive adjustments, and no decisions or changes that lead towards this ideal future vision.

There is no Reverse Engineering.

I always explain it like this. When you want to build a house, you don't begin by picking up a hammer, you create a blueprint. This is the architectural plan to follow to ensure that you end up with your vision. That is what I mean by "Reverse Engineering." Think this is just mere theory? Why, you are already an expert!

Consider your patients and your treatment plans—you begin with a vision of the end result, then you move backwards to know where to start, and then you begin on the foundation. Anyone can throw on some composite and cement the crowns. But you have to ask yourself how will what I'm doing to this tooth impact all the others. How is the bite going to work and how is all of this going to look? There are so many considerations and each one is "reverse engineered."

Of course, way too many dentists are still practicing one tooth at a time, step-by-step dentistry without any vision or Reverse Engineering to their treatment plans. Naturally, they are getting exactly what they are creating for themselves and their patients—not much.

Done right, Reverse Engineering your practice is really no different than the steps you employ to reverse engineer a treatment plan.

Your business must be constructed based on the way you want it to be; what I call "the state of ideal." Anything short of that is your own fault—at least once you know—and now you do.

Here is the good news. Reverse Engineering isn't just a fancy word or a made-up business term. It is a specific process and formulaic approach that will allow you to truly customize and make your practice your own while keeping intact the integrity of sound business principles that will never fail you.

Do you see yourself in one of these spots?

- You are looking at a short horizon of a few years and you want to bring in an associate so you can transition to Sleep Dentistry, or some other specialty. Or, you want to work fewer hours in the practice you own, or you want a few million dollars more in income before you can hang it up and go home, or maybe you never want to quit.

- You are just starting out or midstream in your career and you don't want to wait another couple of decades to figure it out. You don't want to wait to have a full-time income by profiting as a business owner and working a part-time schedule without stress or much effort.

To each their own—and that's the point! I don't care what your goals are, just that you have them and then you take responsibility to deliberately reverse engineer them to success. Now that you know Reverse Engineering is the ultimate secret to building the practice business of your dreams, I'm going to give you the 3-Phase Formula to show you exactly how to do that.

### Reverse Engineering

"A goal without a plan is just a wish."
– Antoine de Saint-Exupery

The worst part about being your own boss is also the best part—no one tells you what to do. Sounds so good, doesn't it? Except when you are trying to figure out what to do next. Or first. Or change. Or improve.

Who doesn't love to be in charge? A person without any direction, plan, or goal, that's who.

Think about it. How can you possibly know how to make decisions or adjustments to your business if you do not have an exact place where you want to end up or a specific goal you are trying to achieve? It's like building a house without a blueprint or creating a treatment plan without a process or doing anything without the clarity of a vision of the future.

If you are just going through the motions, you are going to be disappointed, you are going to end up further from your goals, and most certainly you are going to work way too hard for what you are getting. If you first know what you want, you can create it.

The entire point of Reverse Engineering is that it prevents waste, frustration and detours along your journey. You have to have a plan that's been reverse engineered based on your vision for your practice, or it's never going to happen. This is far more important than you will ever realize unless you actually embrace and own this concept.

This technique applies to all aspects of your way of doing business, leading your team, growing professionally, making money, practicing dentistry—really everything in life. As I said earlier, even the way you treatment-plan your patients comes down to Reverse Engineering. But, no one does this. At least, most dentists never think about working backwards from their vision of the perfect practice and plan it down to the tiniest detail.

### Reverse Engineer the Ideal Practice for You

Think of this as a two-part process.

In the first part, with my guidance, you go through the questions in Phase 1 and Phase 2 to identify the ideals and vision that you want to achieve and create your initial "blueprint."

The second part we'll do together, privately, and use your blueprint from Phase 1 and 2 to establish the steps we need to take to create your vision.

# Phase 1

In Phase 1 we will reverse engineer the structure of your practice and your lifestyle. Your practice will only produce financial rewards based on the structure that it has been built to provide.

Many doctors are frustrated with their practice every day because they can't break through a plateau in revenue, but when you look at it, the confines of their practice prevent them from producing more. The only way to grow the practice is to first set the practice up for growth.

Phase 1 includes some questions you need to consider. Your answers will help assess where you are in establishing the practice of your dreams.

It is important to devote some of your valuable time to this exercise. I have found that very few of my clients have taken the time to ask themselves these questions, much less put them down on paper until we did this exercise. Writing it down helps to make it real and that helps you to determine the direction you really want to go.

It's important for you to actually do the work. If you don't, you're not only wasting your valuable time, you're cheating yourself and those you love out of the results you could and should get from your practice.

## Phase 2

In Phase 2 we will reverse engineer your work environment. Here we will deal with what actually happens inside your practice in the "heat of the moment." This is like being on the field, running plays, and scoring points.

## Phase 3

In Phase 3 I provide information and 12 strategies that will help you to attract and retain high-fee and high-profit **quality** patients.

# DR. PATTI SWAINTEK-LAMB
## Preparation Meets Opportunity

"I always knew I wanted to be involved in the health field. When I was in high school, my family changed to a young dentist who was right out of school. He had a vision, a beautiful practice, and he was doing great things. I was amazed by it and I wanted to work with him and his group.

"He hired and trained me as a dental assistant and I ended up working for him every summer after that while I was in school. He was a great mentor and he's the reason I became a dentist."

### The Early Years

"My mentor told me that the best way to realize my own vision was to buy a small practice I could afford before starting a family. I took that to heart, and my husband and I bought the practice of a retiring dentist. It was 750 square feet with two chairs, and in the beginning, I was doing my own hygiene. That was 22 years ago.

"It was hard at first because I had three young children, each a year apart, and my focus was on my family. I was practicing dentistry and I was taking a lot of continuing education. I was working three days a week, but I wasn't super profitable. I wasn't doing great, but I loved it and it was a nice way to balance family and work.

"For years, I maintained that pace. Then, as my kids got older, I did more and more CE and realized that I wanted to do more with the practice. I was ready to make it work. My husband has commuted into the city to work for 30 years. I wanted to make my dreams here at the office a reality, and I knew if I could do that, then he could execute his 'plan B' and do whatever he wanted to do."

## The Tipping Point and Turning Things Around

"2015 was a bad year for me personally and in my practice. I lost both my parents. Then members of the team that had been with me for 10 years began to leave one by one. It was not personal—they each had other opportunities.

"In addition, I felt like I was working for the practice, it wasn't working for me. I paid everybody else before I paid myself. I would look at my financial statement at the end of the month and think, "God, what am I doing here? Why am I doing this? I feel like I should be doing so much better."

"I was beginning to think that it was time to leave dentistry because it just wasn't worth it for me at the end of the day. I knew I needed business knowledge and I considered returning to graduate school on weekends to get an MBA.

"I found Scott when was I was searching for answers during that crazy point in my life. Google kept showing me Scott's name every time I researched MBA programs. One day I listened to one of the videos he had online and I liked what he had to say.

"I finally reached out to Scott and we had that initial phone conversation. I was very drawn to his positive attitude and the things he said. Other people he had worked with told me their stories, and I was like, 'Wow!'

"My husband and I discussed it a lot, and finally I said, 'Listen, I really believe I should do this.' Now my husband is in awe of this whole process. We're both so happy we did it."

## The Change

"I began the LVI continuum in the early 2000s and I focused on TMD and craniofacial pain, as well as sleep dentistry. I've completed a combination of things, along with what I like to call "airway centric orthodontics" and I was at a point where it all just made sense. I was ready to turn it around financially when I met Scott.

"I had never heard about reverse engineering your practice until Scott presented it. We reverse engineered the whole thing, set goals and figured out what we had to do to achieve those goals right down to every hour and every day.

"We also built a fantastic team. I was always lucky to have great people, but I didn't have a team that listened to me.

"Now, here we are in 2017 and I have the best team I've ever had and Scott helped me to hire some of them. They totally get it and it's almost like I'm listening to them. They are on fire for everything that Scott and Kevin say to us. We have our goals, they jump on it, and we've done exactly what Scott has told us to do. It's not hard once you do it.

"Together we have turned the practice into a business that works for me. My personal blueprint kept the things important to me intact—things like my three-day workweek, keeping my family first, and doing amazing dentistry. We serve a lot of patients while creating an experience that reflects my philosophy and the quality of care that I provide."

**Great Results When Preparation Meets Opportunity**

"The sleep dentistry is great. The TMDs are so closely connected. We're helping a lot of people with that. We've made some great connections in our community with some sleep physicians and I'm ready clinically to give our patients what they need.

"In the first six months of 2017, I've collected more than I did in all of 2016. I was amazed when I stopped and looked at those numbers. We are consistent but we aren't crazy busy. We work twelve days a month, and we're making more money than ever.

"We did $125,000 in June and the team got a nice bonus. I even asked Scott if it was the right number because the bonus was so much. I think that is great, and it's life changing for the team.

"We are at $725,000 for the year at the end of June, compared to about $650,000 for the entire year last year.

We are on pace to do over a $1.5 million by the end of the year.

"We have done all of it without adding days, or spending more, or increasing our hours. We haven't compromised our clinical integrity, and we aren't at the mercy of insurance."

**Change is a Good Thing**

"Making these changes has changed my life. Now I feel good about what I'm doing, I'm filled with energy, and I'm happy. It's great to work hard and know you're improving people's lives with your dentistry.

"When the practice is fun and what you want it to be, it's much easier to come in every day, and to be a person that your team wants to work with and go to bat for.

"I also believe the best thing you can do for your family is to be happy with yourself and with your practice. My kids are totally aware of how it's so different for me now.

"I'm also getting back into working out and feeling better about myself physically. It's a very exciting time for me, and I can feel it in every fiber of my being and our family. It's turned the page for us in a very positive way.

"Very soon after we met Scott he asked us to share our personal goals. We have always wanted a beach house, but we hesitated because we were unsure what the future held.

"All of a sudden, it's very different. I know that it is long–term and it's only going to get better. I thought maybe in the next couple of years we could get that beach house, but we're under contract now. We're going to close in mid–September, and I'm just thrilled."

**Advice to Dentists Ready to Go to the Next Level**

"Life is short—try to live in your ideal state as quickly as you can. You can have all the clinical skills in the world but you also need the business knowledge to support them to achieve your vision.

"You have to put yourself in the presence of people who are positive and believe, who are doing successful things, and who have the kind of vision you need to succeed. I believe you have to see what you believe and become what you see.

"What we started with and my vision have changed along the way. Now, for the first time, I feel like the vision I've always had is becoming a reality. That's a good feeling. I have to say that Scott helped me believe that I could achieve it, and now it's really happening."

# CHAPTER 3
## Reverse Engineering — Phase 1

### Reverse Engineer the
### Ideal Practice Structure for You

**40**    Chapter 3

# Chapter 3
## Reverse Engineering — Phase 1

## Reverse Engineer the
## Ideal Practice Structure for You

Here are the questions for you to consider. Take some time to answer them with your top of mind, gut reaction—your visceral thoughts. Once you have the main points answered, take some time to flesh out your answers so you will get the most from this exercise. Remember, you get back what you put in.

### 1. What Kind of Lifestyle Do You Want?

Take some time and think about your "ideal day" from start to finish. Describe where you live, the kind of house you have. Maybe you are working toward the trophy house that you've always wanted. Maybe you've got that and, by golly, you don't need it anymore.

What time do you want to wake up? It's always funny to me that doctors start their days at times where they're not such a nice person. If you're a morning person, start in the morning. If you're not, don't. You get to decide. Patients will only show up when the office is open. Set it up so you're your best self.

How do you want to spend your mornings, your afternoons, your evenings? I have so many doctors with children and they want to pick them up after school. Why not? They're only going to be there for so long. Please do not hold back. Make these goals, these visions, these dreams. You have to let yourself go.

How do you want to spend your evenings? What kind of vacations? What kind of time do you want to spend with family, friends, all of that?

If you don't design this, who will? I'll tell you—your practice, inadvertently by way of your team, by way of your patients, and by way of your lack of discipline. **Other people will determine what your life is going to be like unless you organize it.**

Take a few minutes and jot down some thoughts right now.

_____

_____

_____

_____

_____

_____

_____

_____

_____

_____

_____

_____

_____

_____

_____

_____

## Real Life Success Stories

I just finished the two days of our practice champions training with amazing teams from all over the country. Of course, these are very intimate groups, that's all we do.

We had nine practices here and each one had a different objective. One doctor's objective is to move, to leave where he is now and go someplace else. He wants to live in a different city. And so our objective together is to build up the practice, sustain the practice, have a nice vibrant location and then go and invest in a new location. That's an extreme example, but it is his dream.

Whatever your answers are, they are yours. My role is to help you achieve your dream, not tell you what your dream should be.

Another doctor wants to travel around the world. He wants to do this in three-month increments. We're building the practice to integrate an associate so there will be no income loss when he exits for three months at a time.

Again, that's an extreme example, but it doesn't matter what your objective is, together we can achieve it. You may simply want to be home earlier. You may want to go back to playing golf or more fishing or enjoy more art or more time with your kids. It doesn't matter.

I'll tell you a little story. I had this amazing guy, Dr. McCall from Waco, Texas. Waco is an amazing place, made even more famous by the beautiful TV show with the husband and wife doing the makeovers. Isn't that what you do? Don't you make patients beautiful?

Dr. McCall, an art lover, was uninspired when he came to me. He really did not enjoy dentistry anymore. He was disheartened by what he was doing, and was even considering stopping. He was grinding it out, just doing the dentistry that came through the door because he didn't feel invigorated to do anything different.

He had listened to a lot of people who tried to change him. When we met, I said, "Dr. McCall, we don't need to change you. You're the best. You are who you need to be. What we need to do is bring some life into this practice, and that starts by accomplishing the things on your wish list. We can achieve balance in your life and incorporate some of the things into your life that are important to you outside of dentistry."

There were a lot of things that went into it, but we now have doubled his average months and tripled others. It's a relatively smaller practice that had done from $20,000 to $50,000 a month. We are now doing $50,000 to $90,000. And he's not stopping. But you know what? Every time I talk to him, the money is not the thing that he's excited about. He is excited because I gave him "permission" to work only three days a week. I gave him permission.

I said, "Forget about this. You want to work three days because you want less dentistry and more life? There are seven days in a week, so the only way to have less dentistry and more life is to work fewer days."

We went down to three days and still doubled, even tripled the practice. And he now gets to spend more time with his art and with his wonderful wife. He's happier. And because he's happier, he's now crushing it the days he's in the office. And the team sees a light in his eye, a spirit coming out of him, engaging the patients in a different way.

The first order of everything in life is you have to take care of you. I don't care how financially successful you are. I don't care if you're doing $100,000 a month or $300,000 a month. It doesn't matter whether you're working three days, four days, or five days a week. This is about how you feel. This is about how you act with other people and whether you can be an inspiring leader or not. If you're not inspired and happy and invigorated doing everything the way you want you need to change it.

Make the wish list. Do it now.

## 2. What Are Your Daily Responsibilities Within Your Practice?

I believe 9 out of 10 doctors fail to answer an important question. 9 out of 10—and that means there is a good chance you have missed it, too. The question is, "What is your role within your practice and how does that role affect the tasks and duties you must carry out every day?"

I see so many doctors performing a long list of tasks in their practice that they shouldn't be touching. It could be clinically in the operatory, like preparing temporaries. It could be managing their own labs. It could be dealing with ortho starts. The list goes on. There are so many things, even clinically, that you shouldn't have your hands in. Your hands are valuable. They should be touching dollars all day long.

There are other things that could be on the list. It could be bookkeeping, taking out the trash, opening up or closing down. I'm not saying you have to stop doing this, I'm saying that you have to define it. And whatever you decide you want to do, more power to you. Whatever you say you don't want to do, get rid of it. You have to define your role.

Look at it as if you are your own employee. You are your own associate. What are your responsibilities? Take a piece of paper and draw a line down the middle and title the left column "owner," and then write down what you want your owner hat to look like.

Then at the top of the right column write "doctor" and write down what you want your doctor hat to look like. Now, I can tell you this. The greatest, highest income earning doctors I have do as little as possible and do only what they do best.

Now take some time and describe what you do every day. Describe the challenges you face and what gives you satisfaction at the end of the day. You should be writing down what you want your role and responsibilities to be in your practice, including what you want to STOP doing.

This checklist of daily responsibilities is an essential element of the blueprint we will create.

| Owner | Doctor |
|-------|--------|
|       |        |
|       |        |
|       |        |
|       |        |
|       |        |
|       |        |
|       |        |
|       |        |
|       |        |
|       |        |
|       |        |

## Real Life Success Stories

A very special friend to me, Dr. Mahoney, from Indiana, has a practice that he built from $1 million to $4 million, and he will actually reach $6–7 million this year. He does this with two doctors and some great hygiene. They want to do $8 million, but they will probably need to add another set of hands to get there.

What happened is this. He said to me, "Every time we meet, you get something else off my plate and it goes to somebody else." And you know what? We did the same thing with the team leaders. We took the team leaders and we freed them up and we get only the highest and best use of their time. And then we drop something else down to the next layer of team. But by the way, he was great at this before me. His son is in the practice and is probably the best manager I know. ("Manager" is an understatement because he's more like a CEO and a business executive, but he did the same thing.)

Dr. Mahoney had income breakthrough after income breakthrough by doing less, not more. Let me repeat—doing less, not more. And that's how he's able to produce $3–4 million in a general practice, working hard no doubt, but taking good vacations and having a real balanced life and schedule.

I'll tell you another great story, this time about Dr. LaFrom, whose practice is in Cupertino, CA in the San Jose area. Dr. LaFrom actually helps me a lot with clinical development of doctors who need it. Dr. LaFrom came to me and said, "I want to double the practice and sell out. And I want to do it fast."

We did it in 18 months, start to finish. He doubled it in six months, sustained it for six months, and sold it in six months. And he already had a million-dollar practice that was doing well when he called me.

Dr. LaFrom is a micromanager and he knows it. He's the most detailed person I have ever met, but it affected the team and actually suppressed their potential and their ability to grow. So, we worked on leadership and delegation. We worked on building up team member responsibilities and removing doctor responsibilities.

Dr. LaFrom had great discipline and powered an amazing team already. But he was able to grow the practice more because he got out of his own way and let other people take the reins.

And he has become an amazing mentor and consultant to so many doctors. You should ask yourself if you are too involved in some aspects of your practice and document it so we can come up with solutions that fit your needs.

### 3. How Much Money Do You Want to Make?

I want you to seriously consider the amount of money you need or want to support the lifestyle and responsibilities you've already defined. Determine actual numbers based on today's dreams, and the dreams you have in place for tomorrow. The bottom line is to end up with a realistic assessment of the income you'll need to produce in order to experience the life you want.

Now, let me explain this. You want to pay for your kid's or your grandkid's college. You have daughters or granddaughters getting married. You want to leave money to your kids or you want to start another business. You may have real estate you want to buy and vacations you want to take. You have second or third homes, or vacation destination things you want to do. You cannot limit this. If you don't plan for it, it's not going to happen.

*You don't take your income and retire on it. You have to create a surplus of investable assets. You have to create wealth in excess of income.*

I always say that doctors have income and therefore they never get rich. Business owners have wealth in the form of profit, monthly profit. And the only way you get that is by Reverse Engineering it.

Don't come to me and say, "Scott, I'd like to make more money." Instead, I want to know how much you want your practice to be worth. How much do you want it to deliver to you? If you come to me with some unrealistic expectations, I will have to tell you that.

You need to have the fortitude to decide to have an adult conversation and say, "To get rich, I need this number."

An easy way to determine what you need is to take your total revenue right now and call that your collections. Then let's play a game. Let's take your collections every month and turn it into your income.

I do it all the time, but it's easier to do when the practice is not doing well. If you're already doing $1–3 million, obviously it's a little harder. If your personal production is $2-3 million, then, obviously, it's a little harder. What if we took your personal production and made that your personal income? That's a very worthy goal.

But I need you to decide on the money that you want. You're supposed to be writing it down, by the way, right now.

So, you figure out how much you need to live for the year and start with that number. Maybe it's $200,000, $300,000, or $400,000. Then add your retirement savings to that number in order to achieve your wealth goals. If you want $2 million in 10 years, you have to save another $200,00. Now add that to your list. Then add in extras for your family, your philanthropies, for your charities and all the other things you want to do.

It may help you to create categories for your business (operations, equipment, staff, training, etc.) and personal (housing, travel, dining, retirement, savings, etc.)

The bottom line is to end up with a realistic assessment of the income you'll need to produce in order to experience the life you want.

_____

_____

_____

_____

_____

_____

_____

_____

_____

_____

_____

_____

_____

_____

_____

_____

_____

# Real Life Success Stories

I'll tell you another great story. Dr. Handel is from Pennsylvania. He is a very tenacious and disciplined person, somebody I really look up to. He's a great student. He reminds me of my martial arts days where I was a "master" like I am a "master" in dream fulfillment. Although Dr. Handel can teach this stuff, he listens and seeks advice from me, the "master" and then he follows the plan.

Dr. Handel had a great practice, but it kind of got away from him. Even though he was earning good money, he didn't like the way he was earning it. It was very insurance driven. He had gotten a couple of doctors and it just wasn't working out. He was carrying the load for everybody else.

So, we downsized. We got rid of everything. We simplified his life. We fired the insurance and then we basically restored his practice to his original vision of concierge care and individualized patient relationships. His team is amazing, and you know what? His practice has exploded. And he's replaced his income with profitability. He's basically doubled his income with excess profit from the practice.

Now he's reached an amazing spot where he's integrated a great associate, a future partner in the practice, that he's going to use as his semi-retirement exit strategy.

But he didn't do this accidentally. He said, "I have two daughters. I want to spend more time with them. They're both going to be in college soon. I want to fly wherever they are every single month and visit with them. I want them to have amazing weddings. I want to take my team on vacations."

He laid out a plan and he's doubled his income to nearly a million dollars. And he will surpass that this year.

Every time I see Dr. Handel's accountant he just can't believe how the revenue keeps growing. This time he said, "I can't believe it. Every year there's more and more and more." I told him, "Let me tell you how much it's going be this year." And he said, "Oh, I just don't know. I've never seen a general practice do that."

Dr. Handel's accountant is great, but I have never met an accountant who has ever made any money. All they've done is manage other people's money. They just manage other people, so they don't understand the dynamics of making money.

The bottom line is, you don't get advice about business from somebody who is managing money, only from somebody who knows how to make money—and that is me for you. Well, that's why you're reading this book!

### 4. What Kind of Schedule Do You Want to Have?

I love this one. I mean, it's probably my favorite just because it's so easy to do. This involves how many hours you want to spend on your practice—both working IN your business and working ON your business.

For example, how many days a year you work, what time you arrive at work, what time you leave, and so on. Write this out and describe your perfect schedule.

Once you figure out the days you want to work, we can figure out how much those days need to be worth. How do we do that? Well, take the conversation we just had. We take the money conversation and then we take the days you want to work and we divide the number.

Amazing, isn't it? Math is so amazing. And simple math makes people very, very wealthy. It makes dentists enjoy what they do because it gives us a laser focus target at exactly how much the practice needs to produce for them.

Do you see what I just said? *How much your practice needs to produce for you.*

Do you ever think like that? Or do you just think how much you have to produce for it? That's not very exciting.

I want you to write out your schedule right now.

And by the way, I have amazing clients on the phone. All my clients are amazing, because they're listening, because they study, and they never stop learning. And they've done this time and time again. But you know what? Every time they do it, they make different decisions.

In fact, I was just talking with an amazing doctor today, I'll talk to you about later. He's absolutely the best because he doesn't care. He keeps taking more days off his schedule, more days off the schedule every year. And he makes more money in fewer days. But that is not going to happen unless you force it to.

Now if you love the work, that's fine. I didn't say you have to work less. I'm saying that you have to define it.

You take your schedule and you write down, "This is when I'm going to come in. This is when I'm going to leave. This is how many days I'm going to do it."

I have schedule stories that would blow your mind. I have doctors that will take three months off in the winter. Others take one month off every quarter.

The most common schedule that we have is what we call the three-by-three. Three days a week, three weeks a month. And then they take an average of a week off per month.

Now, of course, I prefer for you to work. It makes my job a hell of a lot easier if you'll actually show up to work. But it's whatever you want.

So, think about it and write down your idea of the perfect schedule for you.

_____

_____

_____

_____

_____

_____

_____

_____

_____

_____

_____

_____

_____

_____

_____

_____

_____

_____

_____

_____

## Real Life Success Stories

I have a great, very personal friend, Dr. Pierce, from the New York area. And he was a master of discipline before I met him. His model was a 12-day cycle. He crams in 12 days as quick as he can and then he takes time off.

He has so many cycles through the year and he packs a powerful punch because he is organized and very disciplined. He has a goal of $20,000 a day, but there are always ebbs and flows when you're performing at that high of a level.

But the fact is that he does not color outside the lines. He set up his life the way he wants it. He has a clinical schedule the way he wants it. And the practice does not encroach on his life. He's also a tenacious and avid, maybe even obsessive, clinical student, so he's constantly going to courses. We had to factor that into his plan, too.

Most doctors fail because they do not accurately look at their year. They think they have all the days on the table. They say, "Well, I'm going to work four days a week, every week of the year."

Well, first of all, no you're not. You're going to decide to attend a course, or you're going to go on a vacation. And then family issues come up. You're going to have days taken away from you. You can add days and then destroy the quality of life of your team. Or you can start the year with fewer days and produce more dentistry per day by following my value-based scheduling method.

My method works for any doctor no matter what numbers we need to put into it. I need you to make a decision about this right now.

## 5. What Type of Dentistry Do You Want to Do to Support This?

The next part is probably the most fun. Based on your answers to one, two, three, and four, you can determine the kind of dentistry your practice needs to do to make this vision a reality.

This could involve using associates, partners, and/or more team members. It could include multiple offices. It doesn't matter to me. But we need to know what kind of dentistry you want to do to support your vision. This is such an important question because it determines how satisfied you will feel at the end of each day.

Of course, I attract the doctors with a comprehensive mindset, the doctors who want to have full mouth, overall total body health for their patients. I have many specialists, too. Some specialize in implants and that's all they do. Or some doctors only do sleep and TMJ. I have more private practices. There are all kinds of those popup, cookie-cutter, franchise joke clinics, but then there are also the advanced specialty clinics with great doctors. They simply decided that's what they want to do and I work with many of them.

Let me tell you something. The only way you're going to beat corporate dentistry is to differentiate yourself by what you do inside the four walls of your practice. And that's what we're talking about here. It's YOUR business. It's up to YOU.

Take time out now and write out the kind of dentistry your practice will perform and provide.

_____

_____

_____

_____

_____

_____

_____

_____

_____

_____

_____

_____

_____

_____

_____

_____

_____

## Real Life Success Stories

I will tell you something about a doctor who's very, very unique, and very special to me. He is probably one of the most intriguing and inspiring individuals I've ever met. Dr. Kagan's practice is based in Florida. For decades, he has spent the majority of each year either living in California, or traveling the world, or staying in his beach home in Florida.

And all the while he's practiced dentistry basically four days a month. Four days a month.

He lived his dream practice in Florida for a long time and then he went to California, fell in love with it and said, "Well, I want to be here. What am I going to do?"

So, he set out on a mission to design a patient–centered practice leveraging the work of associates. It's a three-doctor associate model working seven days a week. Now you know that's not always the model I condone, but you understand it's what he wants, so it's fine. He has three doctors, seven days a week. It is a beautiful setup. He provides an amazing patient experience, which I've helped with, and he has a great team. It's 100% team driven. And of course, we are working on more comprehensive dentistry. This is the dental practice he wants, it's what he decided to do so long ago, and he stuck to it.

We're not talking about small potatoes here. We're pacing out at probably well over $4 million dollars this year, if we do things properly.

Now, if you have an owner doctor working all the time, then that average production per doctor is maybe not as great. Most of my primary doctors average over $2 million dollars. In his case, his associate–based practice is doing over $1.5 million per doctor. Do you understand?

Now, we're building up to that so not every month is in that range. But you know, it's a very, very special thing, and it happened because he stayed true to his core principles, his founding philosophy, and the integrity of the vision that he had for his practice all along. He would say anyone can do it, but I don't know. He's pretty special.

I will say that any single dentist can set up their practice exactly the way they want it to be. They can certainly decide on the kind of dentistry they want to do.

You don't want to do any more fillings. Okay, then, why are you? You can send them to somebody else. You can have another doctor do them. You can do them in conjunction with a quadrant of work. You can do a full mouth case. I have so many powerful doctors doing sedation and packing a punch.

The rule is, if it's in the treatment plan, it gets done. If all of the treatment can be done in one visit, that's how it's scheduled. I don't know any other doctor on earth saying, "Hey patient, it's okay. You want us to fix a part of your heart at a time?" No, they don't say that. They go into surgery and they fix it all.

You have to have a different perspective and then engineer a model that's going to allow that to happen.

**Get Ready for Phase 2**

We have now worked on your ideal practice structure and your lifestyle. We will now move on to Phase 2 to Reverse Engineer your ideal work environment.

# THE KEY TO TOTAL CLARITY:
## Your Reverse Engineering Self-Assessment

This ground breaking tool is to help you achieve absolute CLARITY regarding your goals and dreams for your ideal practice.

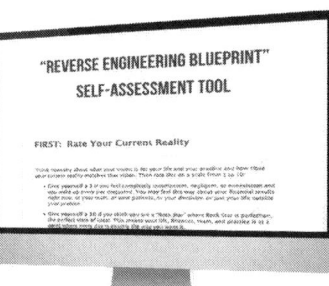

It's totally complimentary, as there's no charge, fee, or obligation. Completing this self-assessment will take no more than 3-5 minutes, but the clarity you'll achieve could be worth tens, even hundreds of thousands of dollars.

## Take the Reverse Engineering Self-Assessment at:

## www.ReverseEngineeringReview.com

# CHAPTER 4
## Reverse Engineering — Phase 2

### Reverse Engineer
### Your Ideal Work Environment

# Chapter 4
## Reverse Engineering — Phase 2

## Reverse Engineer
## Your Ideal Work Environment

Creating the Ideal Environment in which to practice Dentistry is all about leadership. *That means it's up to you.* You have to lead, but not just for the few minutes you are in the treatment room. You have to lead with your mission, your message, your materials, your vision, your language, your team, your diagnosis and your education. You have to live your clinical vision, not just preach it.

To accomplish this, take some time to reflect upon and answer the following questions about your IDEAL Work Environment:

### 1. What is Your Current Patient Experience?

Is your patient experience one that represents your clinical beliefs—does it exemplify your training and your idea of how important oral health and dentistry is in the lives (not just the mouths) of your patients? What could be better, how could you do more?

Here are a few ideas:

- Spend more time with the patient
- Give more attention to the patient
- Add more testimonials into the patient experience
- Provide more patient education
- Share more proof with the patients
- Take more pictures with the patient
- Create more team–driven diagnosis,
  where the team is leading and building the case.

I'm asking you right now to outline what you want and write it down. **Remember, losers listen. Winners take action.**

_____

_____

_____

_____

_____

_____

_____

_____

_____

_____

_____

_____

_____

_____

_____

_____

_____

_____

## Real Life Success Stories

I'll tell you, the greatest patient experience on the planet, hands down, is Dr. Mitchmore from Houston Texas. Dr. Mitchmore is a longtime friend and, of course, client of mine, and really, I would call him a colleague because of the work he does at making patient experiences amazing.

Dr. Mitchmore is a special part of the patient experience he designed. He stepped back and took a look at what he wanted the end result to be with his patients. And he decided he wants to give every patient what he calls, "a large smile." He wants to change their lives.

He doesn't do quadrant dentistry. He doesn't do hodgepodge dentistry. He definitely does not do single tooth dentistry. He does full mouth dentistry and that's it because he doesn't want to be known for anything else.

I believe that Dr. Mitchmore has the highest new patient value in North America. Every doctor is different, but, for example, his new patient value falls within the $32,000 to $38,000 range. Not a patient comes in who doesn't do that full mouth case. Now, don't misunderstand, he's not putting a full mouth on every patient. It's that he's screening the patient on the phone, in the beginning, and creating a patient experience that delivers to him a patient who is going to become one of his special concierge, Life Smile makeover patients.

In this book, I'm providing you a multi-million-dollar opportunity in terms of the future value of your practice by showing you how to analyze and assess and then commit to what you want to change. That's what Reverse Engineering is all about.

Smart, educated, ambitious dentists tell me, "This is what I want." They are the ones I want to work with. They are ambitious, and know what they want. Of course, I'm going to give you advice to make it happen, but you don't want other people's models. I've yet to find a successful doctor who is following someone else's cookie-cutter system who has not made it their own. You simply have to do that. You don't practice cookie-cutter dentistry. That's what the corporations are for. You practice customized care. Well, that's no different than the way we approach a practice.

I'm not saying that you have to follow Dr. Mitchmore's blueprint. I have doctors who do ortho or sleep, or TMJ, or they do all three. They don't do any restorative work. I don't care. Okay? You decide.

But once you make that decision, you have to have a patient experience that creates the outcome. Most doctors are only getting the dentistry that falls in their lap. They accept the easy diagnosis. Most practices are not engineering a patient experience to cultivate the kind of dentistry they want to do.

Now, I'm curious about your list. What do you want your new patient experience to be? What do you want the outcome to be?

This is not just about being nice and making it easy on new patients. This is about what you want the outcome to be.

Do you notice something? Every question I'm asking you is Reverse Engineering. Every question is about working backwards from what you want and stopping where you are today. We will take every one of these questions and layer them together into an amazing Reverse Engineering plan for your entire practice.

**2. How Effective is Your Team at Implementing Your Practice Vision?**

Many doctors have told me, "I have a great team." But when we sit down and talk about it we might agree that they have a great team but they're just not doing very much.

You can have the best people, but are they performing and executing and implementing at a high-performance level? You may have team members who are highly skilled, but they're not working very well with the rest of the team.

You can't have great dentistry, high profits and amazing patient outcomes if you have a subpar team dynamic.

So, go to work, think about it and write it down. I want you to think state of ideal, "if I had the best..."

You don't have to change the people. We're saying if your team was performing at optimal level, what do you see that could be different, better, more improved? What would you change? What would you add? Or, maybe it IS the people.

Ask yourself if your team represents your passion, your purpose, your ultimate benefit to your patients? Do team members convey to your patients the mastery you possess and your clinical skills and priorities of health for your patients? Are they your biggest and strongest advocates? Educators? Salespeople? Or are they just normal ordinary people going through the motions of doing their jobs?

Now stop and describe the current challenges you see in getting your team to make the vision you have for your practice a reality.

_____

_____

_____

_____

_____

_____

_____

_____

# Real Life Success Stories

Dr. Schmidt, from Jackson Hole, is really tenacious, focused, and persistent. She's going to conquer any challenge she faces.

Dr. Schmidt is one who really pours herself into her team. She set out to instill her vision in the team, and then gave them permission to try, and permission to succeed or fail. She also gave them permission to try other things, as long as they continued to represent what she wanted her patient experience and patient outcomes to be.

She is amazing at cosmetic dentistry. They're knocking down one great cosmetic case a week. She often diagnoses a new cosmetic case every day. These cases aren't just three-unit bridges or six veneers. I'm talking about an arch. I'm talking about something special. She's really doing a great job.

As a result, she's had months in excess of $100,000 in delivered treatment on her own. It has grown by more than 50% over last year, and this year I think we'll be somewhere near $120,000 to $150,000. Her completed treatment has increased 50% over one year, and month over month.

She said to me, "I never believed that I could continue to sustain this level month after month after month." And I love hearing that. Of course, it was hard to do before because she didn't believe it, but now that she does, she keeps knocking it out of the park.

And it's because of her team. She would tell you, "It's all because of my team." But she rewards her team with bonuses, life changing bonuses. I won't go into detail, but we are talking thousands of dollars that changed her team's lives.

Why do many practices have turnover? Some people marry, have kids, leave, move, whatever. But what is another major reason many dentists lose great team members? There is only one way to say this. It's because they are cheap. Maybe you think investing in your team's clinical education is enough. But you also need to invest in team members by "sharing the wealth," so to speak.

You have to find a way for the team to win financially. That's what this is all about. Dr. Schmidt is a great example. I can give you many more. Fifty-percent of my clients are female doctors, and I have to say that many of them do a better job fulfilling their visions for their practices and building great teams than some of my male clients.

## 3. How Could You Be Even Better?

Now it's time to talk about you. That's right. Pull out your "selfie" stick. Go look in the mirror and let me tell you something. You now have to ask yourself what can you do even better?

The real winners will take this question seriously. So, critique your own performance as it relates to your own exam with your patients, your own team leadership, your personal engagement with everything you do. What would you suggest to yourself? How could you make everything you do better?

There is no person in the world who can have a greater impact on your success and your future than you. That's the key. That is the key to everything. You hold the most control and you have the most responsibility to continue to improve yourself.

Make a list right now, your wish list. Here are some ideas to get you started:

- Wake up earlier
- Go to bed earlier
- Read more books
- Lose some weight
- Be an inspiring leader

- Show up on time to the huddles
- Review your charts in advance
- Be on time for your treatment plans
- Save more money
- Be more disciplined with your workouts
- Pay attention to your spouse
- Be more attentive when you walk into the operatory
- Be sure to make eye contact and engage the patient
- Talk to the patient, not the assistant or the computer
- Diagnose thoroughly and comprehensively
- Stop being a wimp
- Stop prejudging
- Stop diagnosing the insurance
- Share your passion with the patient
- Be more excited

I don't care what it is. I mean, you want me to keep going? Maybe I should do a "tip of the day" for 365 days of the year. You can set it on your desk. We can all improve. I can give you the list for myself, too.

Take a few minutes right now to make YOUR list.

_____

_____

_____

_____

_____

_____

_____

_____

_____

_____

_____

_____

_____

_____

_____

## Real Life Success Stories

Today we had in our office one of the most successful sleep and TMJ practice teams in the country. They've grown a million dollars a year for three years straight. They started four years ago, so that means every year they grew by a million dollars.

Recently, I was reviewing team results with Dr. Daniel Klauer, who is actually becoming a fairly important person here, traveling around the country teaching about these things in the classroom.

Dr. Klauer and I hit a plateau every time. We hit a plateau at $80,000 a month and then at $160,000 and then at $240,000. I believe the team, as a result of my training, have figured out a way to break through the $300,000 mark.

Now, this is one doctor, doing sleep and TMJ only in a small town in Indiana, working only four days. He says, "I already have $20,000 days at least once a week. Why can't I have them every day." And I'm pretty sure we cracked the code.

The reason I bring this up is because he is one of the most self–critical people I know. Every quarter when we do our special Reverse Engineering training session, he asks, nonstop all day long, "What can I do better?" On this call he said, "What do you think, Scott? Everything I said, what should I be thinking or doing differently or changing?"

**You need to be constantly improving.**

You have to have that mindset or you cannot be a multimillion–dollar business and you cannot be a high–income professional. You're in the one percent if you're cranking out more than $300,000 in income a year. Many dentists make that much, but hide it by spending money, and they're wasting money all the time. Actually, just because you avoid paying taxes doesn't mean you're not making $300,000 a year.

All my doctors are in the top 0.1%. When you climb over the half million-dollar level you can keep going up, up, up. In order to do that you have to have someone looking at your life and practice in detail, someone who can put it under the microscope and analyze what you are doing. That's the only way it happens.

### Did Someone Say "Coach"?

How do the best athletes stay in the game so long and keep winning, and winning, and winning?

It's because they have a coach. They have somebody they trust. They have somebody that's "been there and done that." They have experienced it and they have a lot of knowledge and experience to share.

Feel free to check it, but there is no other person who helps more doctors at a high-income level, a higher average personal profit per practice than I do. And that's why, of course, we continue to have great breakthroughs.

I've given you a lot to think about, but, honestly, it's just scratching the surface.

When you finally take the step back to Reverse Engineer your practice and dig deep to answer these questions about what you truly want to see happen with your practice and with your life you will see the potential for your dream to become reality. Your potential for growth and your fulfillment grow exponentially.

This isn't just a theory. I've talked about multiple doctors just like you who've experienced this kind of results by taking the steps and answering the questions I covered in this book. Doctors like Dr. McCall from Waco, Dr. Mitchmore from Houston, Dr. Kagan from Florida and California, Dr. Schmidt from Jackson

Hole, Dr. Swan from Pennsylvania, Dr. Klauer and Dr. Mahoney, both from Indiana, and so many more.

For me, these are daily stories and that is why I have this expectation for you, too. It is just like when you have an expectation for your patients because they decided what they wanted.

It's all about either fitting your life into dentistry or fitting dentistry into your life. That's what we want to do. These doctors were just like you with practices just like yours, but they took this secret of Reverse Engineering their practices to heart. They actually owned it and they did something to change their current situation to create something dramatically better.

It's very important to take your notes and your ideas and turn them into actions. I can take each of these layers of our Reverse Engineering and turn them into an executable thing for you.

## See What 30 Days Can Do

Because you took the time to read this book and actually go through the process with me I'm going to extend a special, limited time offer to you. I want to give you the opportunity to make a significant improvement in your practice in the next 30 days. This is the second part of our training—the Reverse Engineering Review.

You risk nothing by moving forward. You risk it all if you do not. I certainly am giving you a generous offer and opportunity to allow me to help you. I always say the smartest people say, "Thank you," when they receive a gift. Then they consume that gift and they judge whether or not it was worth it.

We have created a website to help you register for this review.

Go to **www.ReverseEngineeringReview.com** to sign up.

You will first complete a self-assessment to see where you currently are and what is left to accomplish. For applicants who qualify, I will then conduct over the phone a thorough, one-hour Reverse Engineering Review. During this call, I will identify at least three opportunities where you can make significant breakthroughs in your practice within the next 30 days, and I'll help you with them.

If you take action on what I suggest, I will guarantee you'll experience dramatic, positive changes that make a real impact on your practice and on your life. I can say this with absolute confidence because I've seen it happen over and over again with doctors all across the US and North America, from coast to coast, from shore to shore.

Based on my private consulting rate, the value of this Reverse Engineering Review really is thousands of dollars. Let's just say that I'm making a lot of money each day because I'm making doctors a lot of money each day. My rate would be at least $1,000 and probably more like $5,000 or $10,000.

But those who qualify can rent my time at no charge because I want to help as many dentists as I can. This also gives me the opportunity to get more insight into how motivated doctors like you really think. I want to keep my hands in the trenches just like you keep your hands in the patients' mouth. And at the end of the day, if we're going to grow a relationship together, the only way to do that is to test it out first.

There are no strings attached for qualified, serious people. In our review, I'm going to take the notes that you've made and help you turn them into reality.

Once we have worked together to build the blueprint of your vision for your life and practice, we can supercharge and leverage our work to attract more high-fee, quality patients to your practice. I explain how to do that in Phase 3, next.

# DR. BRIAN HANDEL
## Time for a Change

"I've been in general dentistry for 30 years and I've owned my own practice since 1990. I put in a lot of effort and the practice was running well.

"I enjoyed the work I was doing, but I wasn't enjoying the income that came with it and my lifestyle wasn't satisfying. It became frustrating and less fun. Although I loved the profession I reached a point where I plateaued and could not reach the next level.

"I had worked with many, many consultants and practice management groups, but their approach seemed very boiler–plated and nothing new; they would help me get one, two, or three steps better, but I wasn't reaching the point I envisioned.

"It became even more frustrating because it seemed like there wasn't an answer out there. That is when I decided to search for a different answer.

"I found Scott and the change in my life has been dramatic. I have learned from Scott how to customize my practice around my strengths and the life I want to live and how to practice on my own terms.

"After talking to Scott just two or three times it seemed to me that he could read me better than anyone has read me before. He asked all the right questions and really delved into what my needs were. He even helped me recognize needs I didn't realize I had.

"So, I gained clarity after speaking to Scott, which I've never had in this way when it came to my practice. And he also gave me clarity with my personal life and my financial life, which is vital because each area impacts the other."

### A Great Practice Can Still Have Challenges

"We had several challenges within the practice. One of the first challenges was consistent treatment acceptance and getting patients to pay for their treatment in full.

"Another was getting the team to buy in, follow my vision and become almost self–motivated so that I could count on them to take the practice on as though they were owners.

"I also had associates in the practice, and I wasn't totally comfortable with scheduling, case acceptance, and my role. It sometimes seemed like I was the only one doing the dentistry.

"Scott helped us implement some team systems and simplify our processes. He helped us create a robust business where I am not the one doing all of the work.

"One of the main things we accomplished was empowering our team and allowing them to assume many of the responsibilities that were not an option before.

"We now delegate anything we can legally delegate and give them the responsibility and some power in the practice. And we pay them significantly more to assume these responsibilities with our bonus system.

"Since they've become empowered and motivated by this, they've taken the practice over. They basically run my practice in a way that aligns every idea I have about what we want to achieve long–term and short-term, and it's like running a corporation. I'm the CEO and everyone else runs it underneath me, which is tremendous.

"It is important to me that the team experiences a victory and that our changes have a life–changing impact on each team member. It's extremely gratifying to hear how the bonus money they earn enables them to enjoy life experiences they never thought they would have.

"Empowering and rewarding each team member encourages them to stay with the practice and grow their career. The system also creates a trickle–down benefit that has a positive impact on our patients getting healthy.

"We have changed our hours significantly and now work the hours that we want work. Our patients aren't dictating the way we work anymore.

"My time, which is the most valuable thing I have, has become mine again—I work when I want to work, I don't work when I don't want to work. I spend time with my family whenever I want to. I take vacations when I want to, as long as I want to. And I never feel it financially. So, that's been great.

"My most important win is my family time, my personal time. That goes along with making my staff happy and successful. Those two things are probably the most important things I've ever achieved.

"It pleases me that both of my daughters have expressed how much they valued the vacation experiences we have been able to enjoy together since the changes were implemented.

"We used to work from 6:30 AM to around 6:00 PM two days a week, and from 10:00AM until 8:00 PM two days a week. On the two late days I didn't get to spend much time with my family, which was annoying. Also, we seemed to work harder.

"We changed those hours significantly—now we start at 7:45 AM and we finish by 3:00 PM. We have our afternoon huddle and everyone's out of the office by 3:30 PM.

"The most amazing thing about that is we decreased our hours and made them more convenient for us, and the practice numbers have dramatically increased, which I did not expect."

### Putting Scott On My Team Changed My Life

"My income has almost doubled, which is more money than I ever imagined having.

"I live a pretty simple life, but I like to travel and there are certain things I love to do with my kids and money is not an issue.

"My retirement savings have grown rapidly. When I look at the balance in my account at the end of the month, it amazes me how much I put into it. It was dramatic the last time Scott and I looked at it together and realized the amount we project I will have by the end of the year.

"I never imagined having that amount of money in the period of time that I started saving the way Scott taught me how to save and the way he taught me how to invest. All I can say is it amazes me.

"It's dramatic—I almost laugh when I look at the balance on my statement. It's a great feeling. It's a great feeling to look at that and it just makes you feel like you could do anything.

"I read everything that comes across my desk and I search things on the Internet, but Scott is teaching me things that I've never heard before. He not only teaches it, but he also helps me understand how this is going to help me by explaining it in simple terms.

"He taught me how to do this much like I treatment plan and get case acceptance from my patients. I treat my patients the way Scott treats me, and that trickle–down works on every level. I do it with my kids and I do it with associates that I come across in everyday business. It's amazing. And that's made a big difference in my life.

"The only thing I regret is that I didn't meet Scott years ago. I have a great associate with me now and I'm hoping to instill all of this in him so that his career is even more successful at an earlier age.

"I'm excited to phase myself out of my practice in the next five years and become a partner, half–owner or maybe even sell out completely and work as an associate.

"I love what I do, but I would love to hand off the baton, let my current associate manage the practice and just do the dentistry I love to do. I would love to spend the extra time with my family and travel and do the things that I'm kind of doing now, but even more so."

## You Can Do What We Did

"To anyone who is sitting on the fence, not sure what to do, I would say, 'You know what? You don't want to hesitate, just like you don't want your patients to hesitate on their treatment because you understand why they shouldn't. You really need to look at your career, see where you are.

"I think you need to be decisive, to have goals, to not settle, and to certainly seek help and collaborate with somebody who can capitalize on your strengths and offset your weaknesses and get you to your goals faster.

"If you're not where you want to be, you should not hesitate to work with Scott. It will dramatically change your life.' I think that's such an important point that I tell my associates all the time, and I think if they took it to heart it would make a huge difference in their lives."

# THE KEY TO TOTAL CLARITY:
## Your Reverse Engineering Self-Assessment

This ground breaking tool is to help you achieve absolute CLARITY regarding your goals and dreams for your ideal practice.

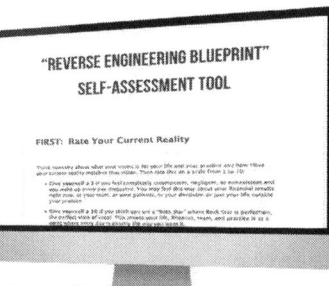

"REVERSE ENGINEERING BLUEPRINT"
SELF-ASSESSMENT TOOL

FIRST: Rate Your Current Reality

It's totally complimentary, as there's no charge, fee, or obligation. Completing this self-assessment will take no more than 3-5 minutes, but the clarity you'll achieve could be worth tens, even hundreds of thousands of dollars.

## Take the Reverse Engineering Self-Assessment at:

## www.ReverseEngineeringReview.com

# CHAPTER 5
## Reverse Engineering — Phase 3

### Reverse Engineer
### to Attract More High-Fee Patients

# Chapter 5
## Reverse Engineering — Phase 3

### Reverse Engineer to Attract More High-Fee Patients

Now, as you know, you are in an industry where everything, quite literally, is relative. "High fee" means different things to different dentists. So, whatever it means to you, these principles and ideas and strategies will still apply.

There are 3 immediate benefits to making this happen:

1. You will get more patients expecting and interested in complete dentistry that results in higher fees that they are willing to pay and they are excited for the outcome.

2. You will see your case acceptance conversion dramatically increase during the treatment conference and immediately after. When case acceptance speeds up, you know what else accelerate—your cash flow.

3. You will feel the effects of creating aggressive and proactive referral stimulating patients because they will all be talking about what you are doing for them. Instead of trying to get someone to tell their friends about their cavities or cleanings, they will share about their smile and the life–changing dentistry you provide.

The most amazing high–fee, profitable, and FUN and profitable dentistry can be yours and you can have the schedule you want, doing the procedures you love. All you have to do is master the art of attracting, wowing, and getting acceptance from the highest quality, most appreciative patients in your city who are willing to invest in their dental health.

Okay, now let's move on to how to make this happen.

## 12 Actions to Attract and Retain High–Fee High–Profit Quality Patients

Here are the exact steps to take to attract profitable high-fee cases from quality patients that appreciate the approach to complete dentistry that you take in your practice.

I have intentionally made it a point to make each of these items something you can actually **do**. These aren't ideas, they are **actions**.

## 1. Showcase Studies and Stories on Your Website

Use your website to explain what you are about and the transformational results you achieve for your patients. Please, please, please don't just brag and make it look the same as everyone else. Be different, add your personality and let patients pick the dentist that they trust and feel comfortable with.

Remember: if they don't get to meet you until all the way through their first visit, you are hiding your best asset, YOU, from the world. Stop that. And no one cares about your CE listings or all the distinctions. Sorry, unless other dentists are your patients, *talk about what the patient cares about, worries about, and dreams of becoming.*

## 2. Make Your Website Topics Specific about PROBLEMS and not Dental Terms

Before you sell solutions you must make clear the tremendous potential harm that can come from the problems going on inside someone's mouth. Then, if they call in asking about something specific that you've got covered, you pretty much have this one in the bag. You want patients to identify with something going on that's a concern, not just come in for a cleaning and a visit.

## 3. Emphasize "Complete Dentistry"

You offer "complete dentistry" (or your preferred wording) and not something half–way. You want them to know and understand the big picture of your abilities and the diversity of treatments available. Make sure you speak their language and educate the patient well in advance of their visit. You have to lead by example and explain what the patient should expect. If you don't tell them, they make up their own mind and opinion in advance and that's no good for you.

## 4. Share Patient Success Stories

Go back to all previous patients who have experienced more complex cases in your office and Interview them, let them tell their story about concerns, and hesitations, and how many dentists they've been to before you, and what the outcome and benefits have been. Let them share and then get that in front of every past, current, and future patient. They will learn and believe through listening to others.

## 5. Relentlessly Ask for Referrals

Each and every patient is a source of dozens and dozens of referrals. Ask them for referrals and give them the tools to do it. Social media, person to person, through their emails, in the homes and their kids' schools and activities, and at their jobs. Spend the time to get to know your patients and do something to create momentum and make it easy for them to talk about you.

## 6. Partner with Other Dentists and Healthcare Professionals

Be more diligent seeking dentists who have the opportunity to send you referrals. There are general dentists who will refer to you and there are pediatric dentists who have a giant list of parents, who are not their patients, they might share. Also seek referrals from other healthcare professionals who serve the same kinds of high quality patients that you serve.

## 7. Reactivate Past Patients into Exams—Not Hygiene

I see so many people work so hard at throwing money into recall, recall, recall, and there are times and models where this is good, but it is literally no return on investment. Instead, you should be screening your past patients as well as your new patients. If they haven't been in for some time, treat them like they have never been in.

## 8. Offer Special Educational Information

Provide more information to your patients on specific procedures—through email, newsletters, surveys, or even in office events like seminars or open houses 9. Make sure Every New Patient is getting the COMPLETE Picture of Your Practice. Do this long before they ever sit down in the chair. They should read patient stories and learn about the "possible" problems many average patients face so they are not so surprised when you bring it up. Education, education, education.

## 1. Live by This Motto:

"Case acceptance is achieved and won BEFORE the battle is ever fought and the fee is ever mentioned."

## 11. Present Complete Dentistry

Please, please, please, do not prejudge your patients. Do not sell them short and do not rush through explaining the "continuum of dentistry." You must walk them through maintenance, function, and esthetics. Most dentists do not sell more complex and higher fee and profit cases because they do not give the patient a chance to say yes. Share your vision and let them decide.

## 12. Make Hygiene a Production Department

Most dentists do not block their own schedules to even come close to their stated goals and objectives, let alone their hygiene schedules. They should be weighted in production value and specific services and procedures just like a dentist. This will result in more interested patients because the more work they have done in one area the more they will become comfortable doing what's necessary to complete their entire mouth.

### Go Through This Process at LEAST Once a Year!

It's CRITICAL for you to rethink this at least once a year, and probably more often. The key is to get ahead of it, not behind it. Be thinking about the future now so you can work backwards into today and be headed in the right direction and progressing towards where you want to end up.

Most dentists show up, see the patients in the schedule and hope there is money at the end of the day. No Reverse Engineering. But we can pick the type of team you have and the patients you serve. Everything can and should be determined, not just accepted and dealt with.

You might have a sense of what you want your practice to be one year from now or a few years from now. You might want to change it based on the reality of what and how it is right now, in this moment in time. The key is that you know what you want first. Determine this and then we can work backwards to align all components and parts of this for your success.

I can promise you, when you start with a blank page and you outline your ideal practice, you will be more excited and invigorated in your daily execution than if you are just grinding it out and living through it instead of taking control over it.

The biggest and most critical way you sabotage yourself is by not enjoying what you are doing or not having things set up exactly the way you want them to be. By Reverse Engineering and deciding what you want you will never feel or act from a standpoint of resentment or disgust.

It is very easy to stay in the same routine and become accustomed to feeling that you aren't focused, engaged or excited by what you are doing. This happens to all of us more frequently than we realize.

If you go through all 3 Phases of Reverse Engineering as I've explained here in this book—you can double your production. In fact, you can usually quadruple your income, because the next $1,000,000 and the collections from the high-fee patients and cases is much more profitable and valuable to you.

Here is why I believe it's so important for you. No matter where your practice is today, the actions you take over the next 30–60 days can make ALL the difference in where you wind up 5–10–20 years down the road.

I know from personal experience with doctors just like you all across North America, that we can easily move you from $200,000–$300,000 to $600,000–$800,000 and beyond. If you are below $1,000,000 its time we take you to the income you deserve and break that barrier. If you are hovering in that $1,000,000–$1,500,000 range, then you are most certainly ready to Double, Double, Double. Why not. You only live once.

For those select few pushing upwards of $2,000,000 or more, why stop? Or maybe you should. I can provide you with a $1,000,000 income net, working 3 days a week and 3 weeks a month supported off a practice doing the volume you describe.

Whatever you want, wherever you are at, I challenge you to push yourself, not to settle, to step up and truly live the Ideal Lifestyle Practice Model best for you.

# DR. MARK MCCALL
## From Associate to Ideal Private Practice

"I became interested in dentistry when a friend became a dental student and showed me some of the lab work he was doing. The artistry and craftsmanship that went into it was intriguing. Later, in dental school, the lab work was one of my favorite things to do.

"After I completed dental school and entered private practice I enjoyed cosmetic dentistry, especially trying to make things look natural. Being able to relieve patients' discomfort and pain, helping them with dental issues, and helping them to feel better about themselves was very rewarding."

### Life as an Associate

"I started as an associate with a very busy practice. He was involved in all kinds of procedures, including a lot of implants before that was even popular. I was thrown right into it and immediately got a lot of experience. I loved being an associate. I liked going in, doing the dentistry, and then going home. I didn't have to worry about the business part of it.

"After a year and a half, the senior doctor asked me to become a partner. I jumped at the chance. We worked out the financing and I took out a fairly big note.

"My whole attitude was different the very next day from the weight of how much money I now owed. My responsibilities also changed immediately because I was going to become a manager and help with the practice and the business. All of a sudden, I had a different relationship with all of the rest of the team.

"The new responsibilities created a lot of stress for me, and I began to not enjoy any of it. It was a struggle but I remained as a partner for 10 years.

"Unfortunately, toward the end of the 10 years, we had started adding a lot of managed care plans. That was a decision that my partner thought we should make. I said, 'I think this is a mistake, but I'll do everything I can to make it work.'

"Because my work became so volume–based my stress level went through the roof. I would get to the end of the month and think, 'I can't keep practicing like this.' I knew there was a better way. So, after 10 years together, my partner and I agreed to divide the practice and go our separate ways."

### Private Practice Struggles

"Until we separated I didn't realize that my part of the practice was all managed care. It turned out that I had been seeing all of the managed care patients while he was seeing the fee–for–service patients.

"I worked with some consultants over the next few years and gradually got off managed care. Essentially, I was starting the entire practice over. I have now practiced by myself for about 20 years with a few periods of success.

"The greatest challenges for me are business and team management. I worked with other consultants three different times. With each one I would have limited success. Even when I felt like I had some really good people to work with we could only pull it together for a brief amount of time. Production went up and down.

"The last consultant I worked with suggested that I get on a managed care plan when times were slow. And I just thought, 'What in the world? That's not what I want at all.'

"But it was very frustrating for me to have some successes, see what we could do, then lose it. I always felt like I had the potential to do way better than I ever have. But I also thought, 'I just don't like being a business owner. I can't keep people motivated.' It was frustrating and discouraging."

### The Last Straw

"Stacy, my main assistant, had been with me for 12 years. About a year ago I told my wife that if Stacy left I would retire.

"It was funny, a few months later Stacy told me that she and her husband were going to move. I thought, 'Oh, no. I'm nowhere near financially ready to retire. What am I going do?' I was pretty discouraged, but I knew I had to keep moving forward with the practice.

"Around this time I got several things in the mail from Scott. I think the third time I got something it was about a free book. And I thought, 'Well, I can look, maybe there will be a bit of wisdom in there and I can get something out of this book.' I had never heard of Scott but I got the book.

"After I ordered the book someone from Scott's office called and said to my wife, Kim, 'By getting this book, you can also get a consultation with Scott.'

"I remember Kim coming and asking me if I wanted to do that and I thought, 'Oh, okay. I guess I will.' I was really at a point where I felt like I needed something. I was looking for some direction and some sort of hope that things could be better. It was just the circumstances—of me and my practice and losing an incredible assistant that been with me for 12 years—that motivated me to take a chance and hear what Scott had to say."

### Why Take a Chance With Scott?

"I identified completely with Scott's philosophy. He believes, as I do, that it isn't about the dentistry. It's about relationships with people and preserving and preventing disease.

"It's about preserving your own health, too, while truly caring for the patient and getting your patient to good health. Although I felt my team and I had this philosophy, now I think perhaps it wasn't emphasized enough.

"You always want people who can bring out the potential they see in you, and I did feel like Scott was genuine with what he told me. I thought, 'Well, this is my opportunity.

This is what I've been looking for." Our philosophies definitely meshed so it was not a difficult decision to make."

## Change Feels Good

"I was reading a quote from Helen Keller this morning and it said, 'What's worse than being blind is to have sight and no vision.' And it made me realize that for a while I had lost the vision of what I always wanted my practice to be.

"I know that I can't be excited about a practice that doesn't match my view and philosophy of what I want to achieve.

"Scott helped me to verbalize what I wanted out of my practice and my business and that was definitely a vision. He has helped to reinvigorate and refocus the practice and helped me to focus my time on the things I want to do so I can be more effective.

"He hasn't changed me, he's helped me to identify what I really wanted for the practice and myself, and everything else has fallen into place.

"Now I engage more with my team and pay attention to what I'm doing every day. It's a simple thing and it comes down to your attitude and enthusiasm about what you're doing. If you really care about it you're going to have enthusiasm even if you have a laid back personality like mine. That made an enormous difference to me.

"I've always known if the doctor has a good attitude it has a positive effect on the rest of the team. I knew that I needed an adjustment, so just that very little thing made us start to build momentum extremely quickly.

"We also began using our intra-oral camera more than we did before and it has made a huge difference in our treatment planning. You don't have to sell the patient on anything because they can see it. You show them a picture and they say, 'Wow. That looks terrible.' That's made an incredible difference.

"I know it is inevitable to lose some team members over time, and that's another reason why the business systems Scott has had us implement are so important. And, of course, training and rewarding our team members gets them on board and encourages them to stay with the practice.

"When we began Scott asked me, 'What would be your ideal way to practice?'

"I was kind of kidding about it, but I said, 'I think I would just like to practice Monday, Tuesday, and Wednesday.' And that is one thing that I've started doing.

"My mindset is different when I concentrate on only the main production days of Monday, Tuesday and Wednesday. We are beginning to build the practice up and we are seeing more consistency in treatment and revenue than we ever had in the past. At the same time I have increased my personal time away from the practice and that's been wonderful. It is really amazing how fast it has happened.

"And because we have been producing and collecting more we've been able to do some things to the office. We've been doing some remodeling and renovating that we've wanted to do for years. When there's extra money, you don't worry about how are you going to make it every month. That affects your attitude about everything.

"I have zero managed care patients and it's all working. I'm looking forward to the future and completion of my vision for the practice."

**Recommendation**

"Find a way to focus on and do the things you are good at, and have interests that you are passionate about outside of dentistry. I can now focus on my passion for the art of dentistry, creating and helping people, and my own art because of the business and team management systems Scott has implemented."

120    Dr. Mark McCall

# THE KEY TO TOTAL CLARITY:
## Your Reverse Engineering Self-Assessment

This ground breaking tool is to help you achieve absolute CLARITY regarding your goals and dreams for your ideal practice.

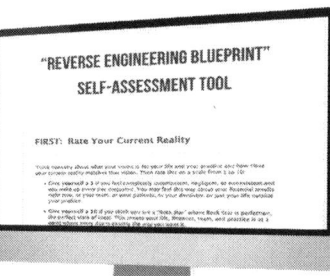

It's totally complimentary, as there's no charge, fee, or obligation. Completing this self-assessment will take no more than 3-5 minutes, but the clarity you'll achieve could be worth tens, even hundreds of thousands of dollars.

## Take the Reverse Engineering Self-Assessment at:
## www.ReverseEngineeringReview.com

# CHAPTER 6
## Reverse Engineering — Implementation

# Chapter 6
## Reverse Engineering — Implementation

### Parting Thoughts

I want to share something here from my good friend Dr. Klauer, whom I mentioned earlier. He says it very, very nicely. He says if you're at a crossroads and don't know what to do next—you're looking for something more out of your practice, your team, your patients, your skills, and your life, but you don't necessarily know how to get there—that's what I'm for.

You don't send your patients home to do their own dentistry. You don't say, "Okay, patient, thank you for coming in. Here's the treatment plan. Go home and have fun."

No, you don't do that. You go to the expert, the best, most qualified, experienced, reliable person you can find, who guarantees their work just like you. I am just like you. I am the doctor of the dental business and you're the doctor of the dental practice. Okay?

Dr. Klauer says his advice would be to anyone who has a lot of ideas and who knows they want to do something more. He says they need to have a business mentor like me.

Don't take his word for it. I'll prove it to you. That's what I'm willing to do.

You don't have to be shackled to the same old results you're getting today. No matter where your practice is, the actions you take over the next 30, 60, 90 days, and the next 6, 12, and 18 months can make all the difference in where you wind up 5, 10, and 20 years down the road.

If you give me the opportunity, I will promise that within 30 days you will see more money in your bank account and have less stress in your day. You will have more peace of mind and you will be invigorated about your practice. And most importantly, you will be excited about the practice you're creating for the future.

Whatever you want, wherever you're at, I challenge you to push yourself, to not settle, to step up and truly live the ideal lifestyle practice, the best model for you. You do not have to do this alone, and quite frankly you can't. I congratulate you for the practice you have built, but what got you to this point won't help you get to the next level.

I would like for you to apply for your free Reverse Engineering Review today so I can help you get to the next level. You've invested time reading this book and analyzing your vision. You made a wise choice to do so. Now it is time to take the next step to get my help on turning these dreams into practical action today.

I can only imagine the charlatans who have lied to you, who talked a good game and promised the world and took your money. Then they delivered nothing but setbacks, losses, and struggles. Maybe you lost team members, or they gave you a big stack of homework. I'm not them and that is not the kind of "help" I offer. I'm not leaving you with homework—I'm offering to do it for you! I'm also not asking for anything other than the opportunity.

I'm not a consultant because business consultants love to tell you what to do and then stand back and watch. I am in the trenches every day, fighting for my independent dentists, helping them with the team, with the patients, doing the work. Trust me. My hands are dirty.

Now, on top of that, I'm not some management person who's going to try to indoctrinate you in what I want you to do. No. I'm going to allow you to tell me what you want and then create that for you. Totally different.

And you won't find that anywhere in our great industry. Many people do a lot of things, but you can only get so far with other people's ideas. You can only take your practice to certain levels with cookie cutter systems from all the other people. You can only achieve a certain amount of satisfaction and lifestyle with a "one size fits all" approach to any part of your practice.

On this review call, I will identify at least three practical opportunities that are easy to implement that will produce a significant breakthrough in your practice within 30 days or less. Many of the Reverse Engineering questions we discussed today will have an instantaneous impact. I obviously cannot give away all of my time, so my offer will have to be limited to no more than 10 reviews within any one month. Slots typically fill up fast, so if you are serious, you will want to get started as soon as possible because it does take time to execute and you want to see those results in 30 days.

Don't wait! Complete your self-assessment and request your one–on–one review call at:

**www.ReverseEngineeringReview.com**

and let's get started!

# Make the Decision that Will Change Your Life

I will leave you with a very important observation. There are two kinds of people in the world. There are people who just stand around, watching things happen. There are dentists who look back at the end of the day and say, "What happened?" And then there are those who make things happen.

And I can tell you this, unequivocally, the successful, the most fulfilled, satisfied, excited, wealthy, dentists practicing on their own terms are decisive dentists who want to win. And smart dentists know they can't do it alone. They aren't looking for someone to change who they are, they are looking for someone to help them to be better for themselves.

I want to thank you for reading this book. I encourage you not to end this day and wake up tomorrow the same as you did this morning. Tomorrow you can wake up with me in your corner.

And I look forward to helping you with your Reverse Engineering Review and taking action on what you have learned about your practice and life vision.

I'm excited to review your answers to the Reverse Engineering questions and go to work on your behalf.

Together we truly can make anything happen. It's all possible. And I have the stories to prove it.

## CONGRATULATIONS!

Congratulations on finishing "The Dental Success Secret To Having a Vibrant Practice That Thrives and Grows Year After Year After Year!"

It's a significant milestone and accomplishment.

So many doctors merely "settle" for a life and career filled with frustration. They accept defeat—living every day struggling against the arbitrary confines of a practice holding them back from producing more, serving more, giving more.

But not you.

You've clearly demonstrated your passion for excellence, for growth, and for positive change that can make a profound difference in your life and in the lives of those you care for.

All because you've discovered and embraced the **Real Secret** to achieving the dreams you hold dear a secret that boils down to two simple words:

Reverse Engineering

It really is that simple. You figure out what you want and you do what it takes to make that happen.

Now the key question:

What now?

What kind of steps will you take on what you discovered?

Moving forward armed with this knowledge requires absolute CLARITY. And achieving a never-before experienced degree of clarity about your Dental Practice and your life offers an adventure you can't afford to miss.

Made in the USA
Columbia, SC
10 February 2018